LIBRARIANS

BY EMMA LESS

AMICUS READERS ● AMICUS INK

amicus
readers

Amicus Readers and Amicus Ink are imprints of Amicus
P.O. Box 1329, Mankato, MN 56002
www.amicuspublishing.us

Cataloging-in-Publication Data is on file with the Library of Congress.
ISBN 978-1-68151-296-9 (library binding)
ISBN 978-1-68152-278-4 (paperback)
ISBN 978-1-68151-358-4 (eBook)

Editor: Valerie Bodden
Designer: Patty Kelley

Photo Credits:
Cover: Wavebreakmedia Ltd./Dreamstime.com
Inside: Dreamstime.com: Wavebreakmedia Ltd 3, 4, Tyler Olson 6, Lisa F. Young 9, Juriah Mosin 15, Emevil 16TR, Krishnadas
Chandrasekharan 16L, Feng Yu 16B. Shutterstock: Wavebreakmedia Ltd 11, Tyler Olson 12.

Printed in China.

HC 10 9 8 7 6 5 4 3 2 1
PB 10 9 8 7 6 5 4 3 2 1

The library is busy today!

The librarian keeps
the shelves neat.
Each book
has a spot.

Jon wants
a funny book.
These look good!

Next is story time.
The librarian reads
books to the kids.

Steve checks out books.
He can bring
them home.

The librarian loves books. So do the kids!

SEEN AT A LIBRARY

chair

library card

computer